THE
★
BIG
TIME

BRYCE HARPER

VALERIE BODDEN

CREATIVE  EDUCATION

BRYCE HARPER

TABLE OF CONTENTS

MEET BRYCE

Bryce swings his bat. He hits the baseball with a solid "thwack." The ball sails over the fence for a home run! Bryce could trot slowly around the bases. But he sprints instead. And the crowd cheers.

Bryce Harper is a star baseball player for the Washington Nationals. He is a powerful *slugger* and a great outfielder. He is a fast runner, too. Many people think Bryce could become one of the best baseball players ever.

Bryce is known for his good fielding and hitting skills

BRYCE'S CHILDHOOD

Bryce was born October 16, 1992, in Las Vegas, Nevada. His dad taught Bryce and his brother Bryan how to hit a baseball. Bryce started playing tee-ball when he was three.

Bryce's family includes mom Sheri and sister Brittany

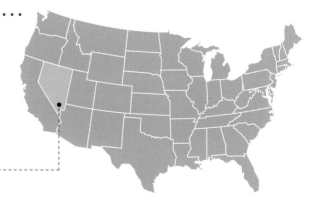

LAS VEGAS, NEVADA

GETTING INTO BASEBALL

When he was nine, Bryce began to travel around the United States to play ball. He played on many different teams. He dreamed of someday playing in the major leagues.

....

Bryce played for the Las Vegas High School Wildcats

Bryce played baseball at Las Vegas High School. But high school baseball was too easy for him. He left high school to get his **GED**. Then he went to the College of Southern Nevada. He led his team to the Junior College World Series in 2010.

....

Bryce's play earned him the 2010 Golden Spikes Award

THE BIG TIME

In 2010, Bryce was **drafted** by the Nationals. He played in the minor leagues for one year and then joined the Nationals in 2012. He was only 19 years old when he started in the major leagues.

· ·

Bryce agreed to play for the Nationals for at least five years

In his first season with the Nationals, Bryce was named National League *Rookie* of the Year! He hit 22 home runs. His hitting helped the Nationals win more games than any other team in baseball in 2012.

Bryce bats left-handed but throws right-handed

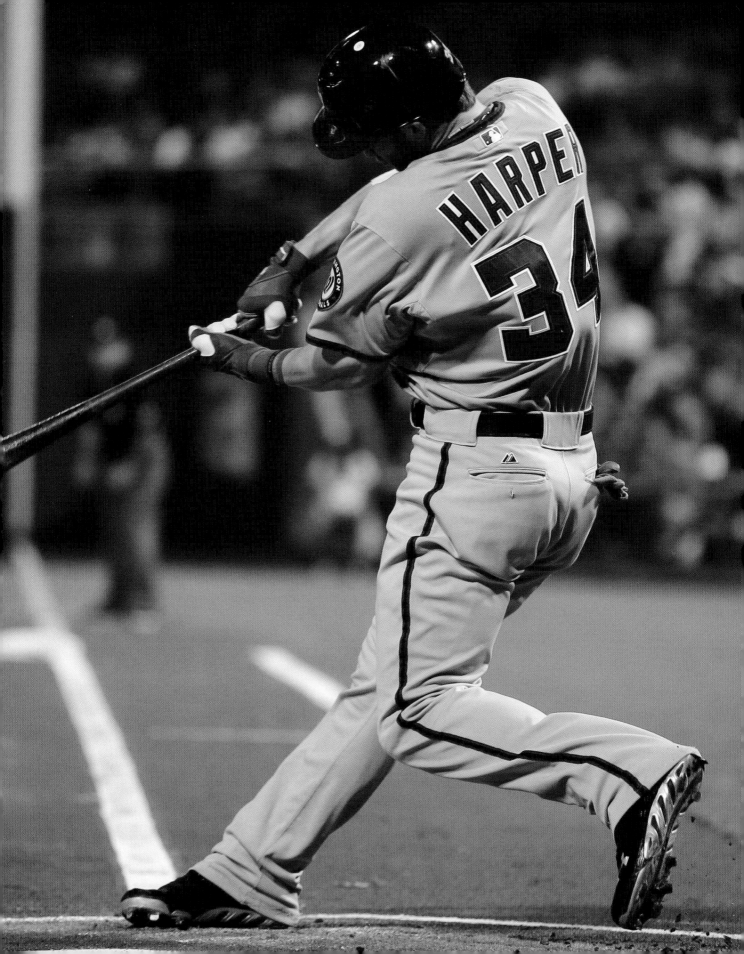

OFF THE FIELD

When he joined the Nationals, Bryce got his own apartment near Washington, D.C. He also got a **customized** Mercedes-Benz car with a rack for baseball bats in the trunk! The back of the car had a curly *W* on it for "Washington."

Bryce signs his name on baseballs for his fans

WHAT IS NEXT?

Bryce signed a five-year deal with the Nationals. The Nationals also agreed to pay for Bryce to take more college classes. Bryce hopes he will help his team win the World Series in the seasons ahead!

....

By 2013, Bryce's talent was impressing everyone in the league

WHAT BRYCE SAYS ABOUT ...

HIS CHILDHOOD

"Everything about it was great. I got to go places, meet people, play baseball against older kids and better competition. I had a great time."

HIS GOALS

"Be in the Hall of Fame, definitely…. Be considered the greatest baseball player who ever lived. I can't wait."

WORKING HARD

"I'm going to go out and give 100 percent every single day, no matter what."

GLOSSARY

customized made special, just the way a person asked for something to be made

drafted picked to be on a team; in a sports draft, teams take turns choosing players

GED a certificate (paper) that shows that a person has learned what he or she would have learned in high school

rookie a player in his first season

slugger a baseball player who can hit the ball very hard

READ MORE

Burdick, Mason. *Baseball*. New York: Gareth Stevens, 2012.

McClellan, Ray. *Baseball*. Minneapolis: Bellwether, 2010.

WEBSITES

Nationals Kids
http://washington.nationals.mlb.com/was/fan_forum/kids_index.jsp

This is the website of Bryce's team, the Washington Nationals.

YouTube: A Bryce Home Run
http://www.youtube.com/watch?v=WLrb9gAwmdA

This is a video of Bryce hitting a home run.

INDEX

PUBLISHED BY Creative Education
P.O. Box 227, Mankato, Minnesota 56002
Creative Education is an imprint of The Creative Company
www.thecreativecompany.us

DESIGN AND PRODUCTION BY Christine Vanderbeek
ART DIRECTION BY Rita Marshall
PRINTED IN the United States of America

PHOTOGRAPHS BY Corbis (BRIAN BLANCO/epa, Steve Boyle, Alex Brandon/AP, Josh Holmberg/Icon SMI, Matt Slocum/AP), Dreamstime (Scott Anderson), Getty Images (Robert Beck/Sports Illustrated, Mark Cunningham/MLB Photos, Mike Ehrmann), iStockphoto (Pingebat), Newscom (Josh Holmberg/Icon SMI), Shutterstock (George Dolgikh, Rena Schild, Debby Wong)

LIBRARY OF CONGRESS CATALOGING-IN-PUBLICATION DATA
Bodden, Valerie.
Bryce Harper / Valerie Bodden.
p. cm. — (The big time)
Includes index.
Summary: An elementary introduction to the life, work, and popularity of Bryce Harper, a Washington Nationals baseball star who won the 2012 National League Rookie of the Year award.

ISBN 978-1-60818-474-3
1. Harper, Bryce, 1992– —Juvenile literature. 2. Baseball players—United States—Biography—Juvenile literature. 3. Washington Nationals (Baseball team)—Juvenile literature. I. Title.
GV865.H268B63 2013
796.357092—dc23 [B]   2013014551

FIRST EDITION
9 8 7 6 5 4 3 2 1